Westside

Westside

THE BRIDGE
of the
Golden Wood

*A Parable on
How to Earn
a Living*

Karl Beckstrand

Yaniv Cahoua

The Bridge of the Golden Wood

Premio Publishing & Gozo Books

Midvale, UT, USA

Library of Congress Catalog Number: 2016949820

ISBN: 978-0985398811

ASIN: B01N0XCPQK

Copyright © 2017 Karl Beckstrand

Illustrations by Yaniv Cahoua & Karl Beckstrand

Other books/ebooks by Karl Beckstrand:

She Doesn't Want the Worms! – ¡Ella no quiere los gusanos!

Crumbs on the Stairs – Migas en las escaleras: A Mystery

No Offense: Communication Guaranteed Not to Offend

Sounds in the House – Sonidos en la casa: A Mystery

The Dancing Flamingos of Lake Chimichanga

Horse & Dog Adventures in Early California

Bright Star, Night Star: An Astronomy Story

Polar Bear Bowler: A Story Without Words

Arriba Up, Abajo Down at the Boardwalk

Bad Bananas: A Story Cookbook for Kids

Butterfly Blink: A Book Without Words

Why Juan Can't Sleep: A Mystery?

Ma MacDonald Flees the Farm

To Swallow the Earth

Anna's Prayer

PREMIO
PUBLISHING

Premiobooks.com

ORDER direct, or via major distributors. Libros online books FREE/GRATIS

There once was a boy who loved to make things. He was always finding better ways to do things. He could even create useful things from objects that others saw as useless.

He always carried tools with him—and he usually had a rope nearby (it was handy for swinging, hauling, and securing things).

One day as the boy was playing along a stream near his home, he noticed an old woman he had never seen before. She was sitting on the bank—looking intently at a mass of branches that the water had piled against some rocks in the stream.

"Hello," said the boy, curious to know who she was—and why she stared so intently at the dead wood.

"Hello," said the old woman, not taking her eyes from the branches.

"What are you looking at?" asked the boy.

"Trouble and treasure," she said.

"Treasure?" asked the boy.

"That wood is as valuable as gold," she said. "But it is blocking the path of the fish, who must feed beyond it down the stream. For them it is trouble." Then she looked at the boy for the first time. "Will you help?"

"Well, I ..."

"If you do, you will have the treasure."

The clever boy needed no more
encouragement. He already had a plan.
He quickly climbed a tree to retrieve
his swinging rope.

The old woman smiled as the boy sat on the bank and took off his shoes. "Excuse, me," he said, turning back to the woman. "How will I know when I've found the treasu ..."

There was no one there—only a splash in the water and the tailfin of a fish going under it.

The boy looked around and peered into the nearby bushes. "Well," he said, rolling up his sleeves, "at least I can help the fish get to their food." The boy waded into the stream and began to gather the branches and lift them on top of the rocks they were pinned against. He was able to wrap his rope under and over them until they were in a large, tidy bundle supported by the rocks that had once trapped them.

As he tied some knots, he noticed eager fish swimming around and past him under his bundle of branches.

Just as the boy was leaving the water, a man with a large sack on his back approached the stream. "I'll give you a gold coin," he said, "if you let me across your bridge."

"My bridge?" said the boy. "Ah, of course! Please come across." The man thanked him and gave him a small coin of gold before going on his way.

Every day after that many travelers and peddlers came across the boy's bridge, and each of them gave the boy gold (which his parents let him keep, since his idea and effort had created the source of the income).

The boy spent many a happy day playing along the stream, watching the fish feed, and earning money to feed his family. He never saw the old woman again.

What did the boy do that helped him to find the treasure? How might you find treasure in trouble?
Problems and needs are opportunities to help and can lead to income. See opportunity in every obstacle. Can you solve problems or serve people? Then you can earn money—even pay for your living expenses and those of others. What if you see a need, fill it, but don't get paid? Are you sure you weren't paid? How do you feel helping someone? Pretty good, huh? (Some people pay with things or via service.) Even without pay, you gain a reputation as a worker, a problem solver—plus you get experience to make you more valuable to future customers (you may also get ideas for products/services that could earn money in the future). Some ideas below may not be suitable for where you live or for someone your age; be sure to have an adult go over these/your ideas before you begin a project (also see local and country business laws). The only guarantee of success is what you guarantee yourself through your imagination, effort, and persistence.

EARNING IDEAS	EXAMPLES
Make something to sell.	Cupcakes, an app, a shoe rack, soap, kites
Clean, fix, or repurpose something.	Bicycles, windows, furniture, appliances, tools
Collect something to sell.	Stamps, coins, books, games, antiques, wood, fruit
Create something to sell.	Photographs, paintings, music, fonts, games, crafts
Grow/raise something to sell.	Watermelon, lavender, nuts, sheep, pets
Recycle for cash.	Metal, glass, plastic, electronics, paper, clothes
Rent things to people who need them.	Property, tools, vehicles, ad space, electronics
Trade things for something more valuable to you.	Toys for games, electronics, clothes, or collectibles
Sell/give something extra you can spare.	Books, toys, games, clothes, gadgets
Sell other people's product to earn a percentage.	Candles, cookies, apps, magazines, ad space
Perform/entertain.	Sing/dance/act/play a musical instrument, do magic
Publish a book/ebook, then ...	Teach classes, speak to groups, write a blog or a newsletter,
Research & share information.	share information via video/audio/Web
Participate/share your opinion for a reward.	Surveys, polls, focus groups, studies, mystery shop
Transport things for compensation.	Pets, people, recyclables, junk, wood, garbage cans

WORK FOR SOMEONE ELSE

Work for a friend, family member, or company—or provide a specific service to many people/clients as a contractor (some work requires a license and/or permits).

As you get older and wiser, your opportunities to earn money increase. There is ALWAYS work to be found or something that needs fixing/improving. Perhaps the only job you see is not the kind of work you prefer; consider taking it for the experience and to network (meet new people and learn of other opportunities).

START A BUSINESS OR FRANCHISE

Solve a problem/provide goods or services that meet people's needs. Seek expert input. Get a business license and tax ID.

• For best results, continue to study business, computers, spelling, grammar, math, speaking, marketing, business law—and the industries that interest you.
• Never sell something that isn't yours unless you have permission from the owners to do so (even art and ideas).
• As your business grows, hire a team of hardworking people (especially those with skills you don't possess)
• Always plan your work; write specific goals and steps! Be flexible and creative. Make house calls. Work. Do your best. Be helpful—even if there seems to be no reward. Find partners with integrity. Budget your time and money. Keep your word. Be positive. Make decisions based on the best facts available (know your industry!). Constantly improve. Take care of your health. Be honest. Be Kind.

TIP: Be sure you can trust the people you work for and with. Signed agreements can help you avoid some conflicts.

TIP: Education can make a great difference in your earnings; it doesn't have to be a college degree; consider trade schools, self study, and apprenticeships. Some companies will train you. (Travel is a great education too!) Each person has gifts that need to be discovered to help others and self. With practice, something you thought you were bad at may become your greatest ability.

SEE: ChildrenEarn.com for information on finding customers, managing money, and moving up in an organization. **Like this book?** *We'd love to get your comments/stars in online venues!*

EXAMPLES

Paper route, walk/groom pets, run errands, child care, wash & detail cars, clean houses, move furniture, chop wood, repair bikes. Some things—like mowing lawns/landscaping, raking leaves, or shoveling snow—are seasonal and can replace other seasonal activities.

TIP: If a company you want to work for isn't hiring, consider volunteering your time. This way, you will gain experience and the company will see what a good worker you can be.

EXAMPLES

Build web sites, sell products or services online, review/rate organizations, clean homes/offices, build things/buildings, promote other people's products/services, connect like-minded people (create an association/newsletter/conference), invent a life-simplifying product, create an app that tracks spending or caloric intake or gives other information, repair tools/electronics/appliances/vehicles/furniture, transport people/things, teach other people to do something you have done.

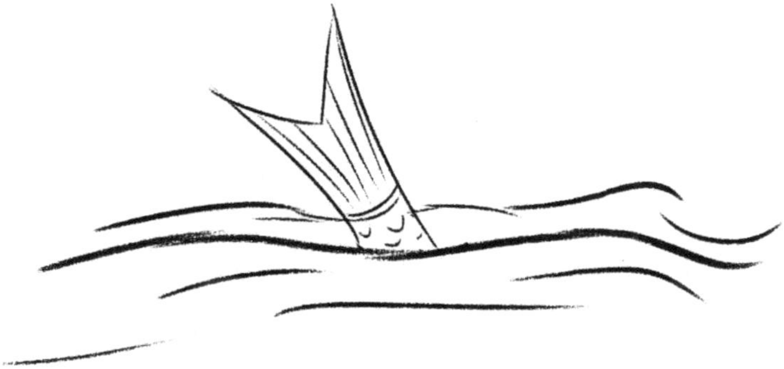